Really
David
Really!

David R Morgan

illustrated by Anastasia Kotelnikova

A2Z PRESS

Really David Really!

This is a work of fiction.

Library of Congress Control Number: 2022908823

Printed in the United States of America

A 2 Z Press LLC

PO Box 582

Deleon Springs, FL 32130

bestlittleonlinebookstore.com

sizemore3630@aol.com

440-241-3126

ISBN: 978-1-954191-68-6

Dedication

*To Bex and Toby
who weave the
magic into all my
minutes and
to all
the wonderful
wonder-making children
that I have taught
Bless you all!*

This Book Belongs To :

_____

What is time but a life understood,
Where there may be disappointment, but mostly good.
My life has been mythical, always something new,
Where all I've made from words is me moving through.

All I've written about is part of me,
Cosmo, Spiders, Ants, Dinosaurs, Winnie,
Whipper-Snapper, and The Magic Tape. Dad grew tomatoes,
Mum grew flowers. See how the magic glows.

Mum and dad now garden in my mind,
Forever together, forever kind.

Their flowers sing,
rainbow fruits sway.
Each magic minute
making
an endlessly
enchanting day.

I recall my great grandfather, Louie, help found long ago,
the Automobile Association that still helps drivers go.

My grand aunt, dancing
Dora DeLise, sang Opera
In concert halls in the 1920's
making hearts swirl and stir.

Now, along comes the axolotls on their aardvarks I see,
So let's follow them to somewhere with mysterious possibility.
There's the beach boogying downside round
As sea with sky dances on the sparkling ground...

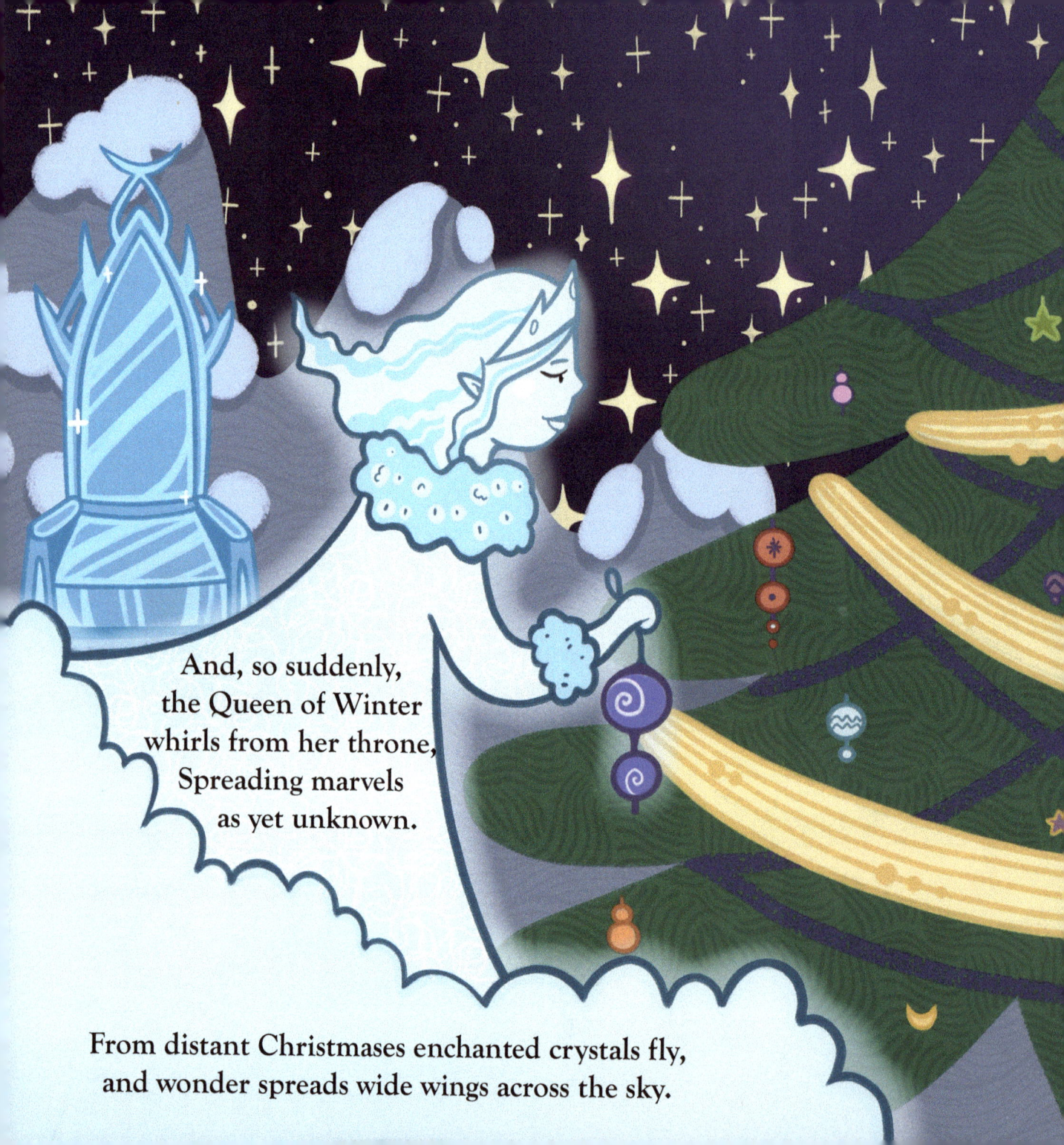

And, so suddenly,
the Queen of Winter
whirls from her throne,
Spreading marvels
as yet unknown.

From distant Christmases enchanted crystals fly,
and wonder spreads wide wings across the sky.

from KANSAS to ELDORADO

I remember, I remember where I was born.
And the incredible creatures at midnight and morn,
Swirling around, they dance and sing, come and go,
Going all the way from Kansas to Eldorado.

In school, I loved chemistry, tweezers, chemicals, tubes, the lab room,
Glass jars, crystals, floor, scoop powder – BOOM!
In the classroom, my invisible pet Griffin was called Stanley.
Pale blue with orange stars, the most colourful Griffin you could never see.

At home, I used to fly a kite so high, asking in letters full and fair,
'Hi God, what's it like up there?'
Then, one Christmas time, turkeys sang cantatas,
Two sausages got married and 'BINGO' – chipolatas.

But see, now everywhere the red roses grow,
Where once there were white blossoms of snow.
There, the silver swan stretches its throat
and out comes a spell-spinning note.

I cherish when you can taste summer in the sky,
Cool drinks, ice-cream, warm sun so high.

And then, when autumn comes our way,
Every luminous falling leaf caresses each minute of the day.

I adore a word that rhymes with spoon,
'I shine at night because I'm a moon.'
I love a book where Bilbo and Frodo see so many things,
Yes, it is my favourite, 'Lord of The Rings.'

My children make me prouder every day,
They mean more to me
than I can say.
Toby's Graphic Design and
Low Girl band,
Bex helping the NHS
beyond what is planned.

Bex dreamed that she could fly,
Like a bird-girl in the sky.
She took with her a diamond spoon,
To eat the cherry pancake moon.

Toby dreamed that he could fly,
Like a magic magician in the sky.
He took a keyboard that played a tuneful trance,
To make the sparkling sun merrily dance.

Sue has been a constant friend,
Always with a helping hand to lend.
A family is a gift from above,
Giving life purpose, lifting it with love.

We must live our lives to be a merry memory,
Not forgotten, always pleased to see.
If you carry a happy childhood forever with you,
Then you have something that will unfailingly get you through.

Yes, and at my great age
I have truly understood,
That it is never too late to
live a happy childhood.
Cosmo cycles around on his bike,
Winnie wheels in her chair,
Wherever I go my mind's characters
create my childhood there.

The End

Queen of Winter

Watch the Christmas snowflakes tumbling._
Watch the magic crystals fly
From a grey and dappled distance,
Way across the far-off sky.

Each crystal in its unique design,
Is sharp with points of light;
Weaving a wonderful kingdom-covering blanket.
Quilted, sparkling, magic, white.

Beyond the Queen of Winter's throne
Wait realms of marvels as yet unknown.

This Stone In My Hand

This stone has taken in everything
Through invisible ears, without reaction.

This stone has sat under the rain's relentless
Attention, unaffected.
This stone has sat under the sweltering scrutiny
Of the Sun, unaffected.

This stone will not speak, no,
Never once in a million, million years-
Never, ever, and yet, sat in my hand right now,
It says everything I'll never need to know.

Snail

Across the lawn at dawn, you see

Shimmering, my silver poetry.

I have no feet, I cannot walk.

I have no tongue, I cannot talk.

Laying my silken sonnets for all.

Composing, beneath the moon I crawl.

Creative with my semi-circular shell

I leave tales for others to tell.

From the Author

To Teach a Life

When I am teaching, I am mainly "Yeehaw' happy
and I teach endlessly in my own styles.
I smile at the pupils; I smile at them all
and more than most return my smiles -
fresh gold seams unearthed to enthrall
and what will be may be, we'll see,
as every pupil saunters into the sunset of their reality,
seeking themselves across life's high plain miles
and yet all the little prospectors, I lasso them all; y
es, spurs and angels' wings, I keep them all.

Endings so separate have the same start;
galloping through pleasure, riding out pain
and all the fragments "Yeehaw' that soar apart,
shall someday come together again.
David R Morgan

https://www.youtube.com/watch?v=0OaZNsJbUKM&list=UUmSMyxoSbzMeR1leR8bC7-w&index=25&ab_channel=DavidRMorgan

To Teach A Life - YouTube

To Teach a LifeWhen I'm teaching I'm mainly 'Yeehaw' happyand I teach endlessly in my own styles.I smile at the pupils; I smile at them alland more than mos...

www.youtube.com

David R Morgan lives in England. He is a talented full-time teacher and writer.

He has written music journalism, poetry and children's books. His books for children include : 'The Strange Case of William Whipper-Snapper', three 'Info Rider' books for Collins and 'Blooming Cats' which won the Acorn Award and was animated for television. He has also written a Horrible Histories biography : 'Spilling The Beans On Boudicca' and stories for Children's anthologies.

For the last 5 years he has been working on his Soundings Project with his son Toby, performing his own poetry/writing to Toby's original music. This work is on YouTube, Spotify and Soundcloud.

Other Books by David R. Morgan

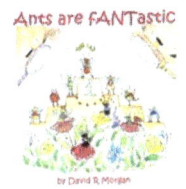 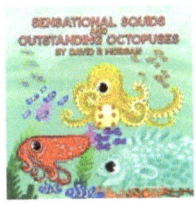  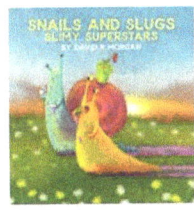 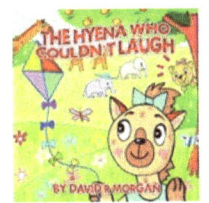

  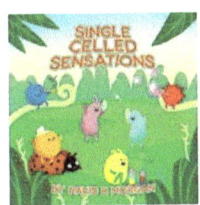  

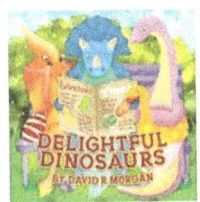 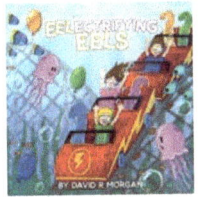   

And many more to come!

More Books by David R. Morgan

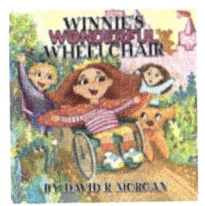 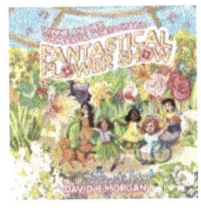 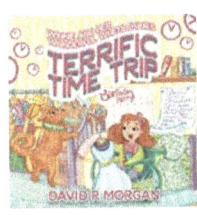 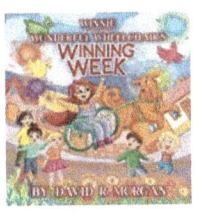 

  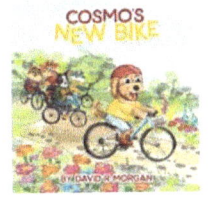 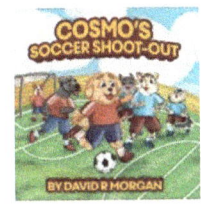 

   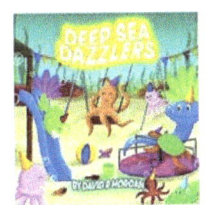 

And many more to come!

www.ingramcontent.com/pod-product-compliance
Lightning Source LLC
Chambersburg PA
CBHW041523120626
46551CB00018B/2552